Presented to

_____

With love from

_____

On

_____

This book is written for Young Ladies from all Walks of Life.
God has you here on purpose to fulfill His purpose for your life.

May this book help you reach your unlimited potential in Christ.

Being a Lady in a Modern World ... A practical guide to wisdom and virtue

Copyright ©2012 Stephanie Garrett, All Rights Reserved

ISBN: 978-0-9814960-3-0

The contents of this book may not be re-produced in any form without prior permission of the publisher or author, except as provided by United States of America copyright law.

Foreword

The work you are holding in your hands by Stephanie contains a rich deposit of instruction in wisdom and virtue of a mature godly woman. As her husband, I know better than anyone of her intense desire to shape the lives of young women for the glory of God.

Every girl and young woman wants to grow up to be what she believes to be "a real woman" – this is natural and by design. And whether clearly stated or implied, every culture upholds a model or standard of what it means to be a "real women." Nowhere is this model or standard communicated more clearly and consistently than through the medium of television, film, and pop music.

The message of our culture is clear. A real woman is a woman who possesses the power to garner the attention, desire, and admiration of men by *just the right display* of her physical assets, or *sexiness*; she calls her own shots always, and is free from the need to live in healthy inter-dependence with others or submission to any authority; she is free from the old-fashioned *bondage* of moral standards of sexual purity and therefore does whatever feels right for her; she possesses a sharp tongue and prides herself on her ability to give anyone who rubs her the wrong way, "a piece of her mind"; her self-worth is directly related to her net-worth and material possessions; and like her male counter-part, she who has the most toys wins.

In the wake of this modern standard of womanhood are hundreds of thousands, if not millions, of younger and now older women who live with emotional and physical brokenness, guilt, disappointment, heartache, and shame, having been misled by the message of our modern culture. Indeed, *"there is a way that seems right to a man, but in the end it leads to death. – (Proverbs 16:25, NIV)"*

Against the message of modern culture lies the enduring wisdom of the scriptures that *"Charm is deceptive, and beauty is fleeting; but a woman who fears the Lord is to be praised. – (Proverbs 31:30, NIV)"* The Scriptures challenge our modern culture's idea of womanhood and reveal that real womanhood, and real power is rooted in virtue, humility, and self-control.

The fact that Paul charged the mature women to instruct the young women is evidence that the younger women would not instinctively know how to govern their lives as it pertains to spirituality, domestic responsibility, sexuality, marriage, and friendship (*Titus 2:3-5*). Young women do not obtain these life-lessons automatically; young girls will not become wise women simply because they grow older. Indeed, young women that are un-taught grow up to become *"silly and weak-natured and spiritually dwarfed women... - (II Timothy 3:6, Amplified)"* who are easily deceived and taken advantage of in life by men, or anyone for that matter, with evil intentions.

If godly women do not intentionally disciple young girls and young women in what it means to be a woman, then television, film, and pop music will. The astounding statistics of sexually transmitted diseases, teenage suicides, un-wanted pregnancies, abortions, high-school drop outs, and hopeless and directionless young women is evidence that our culture's *School of Womanhood* is not producing the kind of future we would desire for the young women in our lives.

What is needed in this hour, and for the sake of the young girls and young women of our generation and the generation to come, is to raise, or more accurately, to re-establish the standard of what it means to be a woman.

This book goes a long way in doing just that. I am proud of this work that my wife has produced, and I am confident that it will bless the lives of the young women who take hold to its instruction.

Tom Garrett,
Senior Pastor, Faith Christian Center – Brandon, FL

Special Thanks

To Amanda Hurst, Rhonda Taylor, Robin Greene, Virginia Williams and Wendy McKoy, thank you, thank you, thank you for your self-sacrificing attitudes, your team work, and your countless tireless and sleepless nights, to make it happen for God's daughters. This wouldn't have been completed by deadline without all of you. Thank you immensely! To Angela Curry, SueRita Gelin, Corliss Cole, and Johnnita Jackson, Angela Tolbert and Veronica Nicholas thank you all for your contribution and for running with the vision. Your reward shall be great. I love you all!

To my Heavenly Father, thank you for choosing me. To my parents, thank you. I wouldn't be here without you. To my Mom, there are no words to describe how thankful I am for everything you've done for me, and for all the sacrifices you've made that have enabled me to be where I am today - I love you! To my loving husband and best friend Tom, thank you for all of your unconditional love and support and for writing the foreword. I love you; you are the best! To Maxwell our son, thank you for being patient while I worked tirelessly on this project.

Love
Stephanie Garrett

Table of Contents

Introduction/You've been Chosen

Chapter 1..11
  Keep It Hot
Chapter 2..25
  The Master's Piece
Chapter 3..30
  Chastity ... 'A Lost Treasure'
Chapter 4..33
  Stolen Innocence (Graphic material)
Chapter 5..45
  Sexy or Beautiful? That's the Question
Chapter 6..55
  Relationships
Chapter 7..70
  Back to the Basics
Chapter 8..98
  Preparation, Never Lost Time
Chapter 9..116
  Dare to Dream

Introduction

"You've been CHOSEN"

Greetings Dear One,

    I write this book from the love I have in my heart for you as a young lady who is in the age group of 12-18 from all walks of life. This time-frame in your life is precious and so valuable because you are growing from a little girl, to a young lady who is forming her own opinions and beliefs.

    If I told you that you have been chosen to do something great and to impact your generation, would you believe me? Or would you think that I had made a mistake and could not possibly be speaking about you? I want you to know that you, <u>yes you</u>, have been specifically chosen and called out. This book was written to give you a blueprint of how to live life skillfully and without regret as a young lady in this modern world.

    As a 42 year old woman, I remember being your age and walking in your shoes, "thinking" that I knew more than I "actually" did and no one could tell me anything.

    On the other hand, I greatly desired that someone who had a real grip on life would show me the way. This book is meant to show you the way with the basics of life. Although my life is a blessed one, I believe I would have been much further along in my life had I been exposed to the information you now have in your hands.

Regardless of your background or upbringing, whether being raised with both of your parents in the home, or being raised in a single parent home, if you are currently in the system through foster care or any other unnamed situation, God has CHOSEN YOU! For some of us, including myself it was easier for me to accept that God would choose someone with a pristine background and upbringing compared to someone who's background and upbringing was not as traditional.

This is FAULTY THINKING. I repeat, this is FAULTY THINKING, because the blood of Jesus was shed for us ALL. God approves of you and has chosen you. It doesn't matter what your situation in life is or has been. Later on in this book you will read the story of my birth as it was written by my mother. (WARNING: it's very graphic material.) This will reinforce the point I just made because it doesn't matter how you start out, but it's how you finish. You, as an individual do not play a part on how things start for you, but you are very responsible for how you finish.

Did you know according to 1Peter 2:9 you are Royalty? This verse states; "But you are a **chosen** generation, a "**royal**" priesthood, an **holy** nation, a **peculiar** people that you should show forth the praises of him who has called you out of darkness into his marvelous light." Therefore dear one, as a young lady, you are actually a **QNT**; a Queen in Training. As you read this book, read it with the revelation that you have been chosen; you are Royalty and, you are a QNT. Having this mind-set will shape your thoughts, your beliefs, and your actions and it will set you on the path of your destiny.

My prayer is that this book becomes an invaluable tool to help you live your life on purpose without regret. May you be a vessel of honor who reaches your generation for Christ.

Chapter 1

Keep It Hot

As a young lady, one of the most important things to understand in life is that life is all about relationship. So often this principle is taken for granted, but the older I get, the more value I have for this way of thinking, believing, and acting.

The most important relationship we can have is a relationship with God the Father through His Son Jesus Christ. It's through our relationship with Him that all other relationships grow, develop, and have their substance. Never allow your relationship with Him to grow dull or stale. Therefore, work to *"Keep It Hot"*. You may say, keep what hot? Your relationship with HIM, that's what. But, if you've never ignited the flame by accepting Jesus Christ as your personal Lord and Savior this may be foreign to you. You may also be in a place where you feel disconnected and have that "icky" feeling even though you are a born again Christian. That is called being out of fellowship. If you are not born again, then this is the most important decision of your life as it will determine where you will spend eternity and the quality of your life here on earth. Choose Jesus Christ!!! Actually, He is the reason that you are who you are and why you will become all that you will become. It's all because of Him! John 3:16 says, *"For God so loved the world that He gave His only be gotten son that whosoever believeth on Him would not perish but have everlasting life."* Jesus Christ died for all of our sins. If you believe Jesus Christ is the Son of God and died for your sins, you can pray this prayer and be born again.

Salvation Prayer

"Dear Lord Jesus, come into my heart. I believe that you are the Son of God. I believe that you died for me bearing my sins for me. I ask that you come into my heart and save me now. I am right now born again."

Prayer of Re-dedication

"Father according to 1 John 1:9 you said that if I confess my sins, that You are faithful and just to forgive me, and cleanse me from all unrighteousness. Therefore Father I confess my sins to You. I repent of sin, and I choose to turn away from it. Thank You for forgiving me, and as of right now I am in right standing with You."

If you prayed either of these prayers and meant them in your heart, you are right now born again or back in right relationship with the Father through Jesus Christ! Congratulations on your decision to make Jesus Christ the Lord of your life.

To those of you receiving Jesus as your Lord and Savior for the very first time:

Welcome to the Family

and, to those of you re-dedicating your lives back to God:

Welcome Home!

How to Start Your Day
with
Daily Devotions

Your relationship with God should be a personal priority. This is not an option. You maintain this relationship by spending quality time with Him daily, through your prayers (conversation between you and The Father), Bible reading, and your constant awareness that He is God; the only True and Living God, and He is YOUR God. This may seem easier said than done with the busy life of being a QNT, but if you make the decision in your heart now, and place a high value in your relationship with Him, the rest of your life will be the best of your life. Jeremiah 29:11 reads, *"For I know the thoughts that I think toward you, saith the LORD, thoughts of peace, and not of evil, to give you an expected end."*

Below are some guidelines that if followed, will get you started in developing your devotional life-style with God:

1. *KEEP IT HOT*

Never let your relationship with HIM grow dull or stale. Do your part to pursue Him. If you draw close to Him, He will draw close to you. This takes effort on your part and a determination to stay excited about the relationship. Although He is God, the creator of heaven and earth, you can't see Him. But He is there, and He is waiting on you.

I remember when I was your age and my relationship with Him had grown stale. I didn't understand what was happening other than knowing that I felt disconnected or had that *"icky"* feeling as I call it. When those times came, I knew I needed to go to church. Sometimes when that feeling was really overwhelming, I would walk by myself when necessary to church (it was only 3 blocks away) ☺. I didn't know then what I know now, that church is an extension of what I do every day and that I could read my Bible, sing songs, or even pray to "feel" connected to Him and get rid of that *"icky"* feeling. My point is that you have to be intentional about your relationship with HIM.

2. *FIND A SECRET PLACE*

- ❖ A place where you can be alone with God
- ❖ A place where no one sees
- ❖ Be intentional about it

Where is the Secret Place?

…any place that you designate as quiet; a place where you can be alone with God

What do you take to the secret place?

- ❖ Bible
- ❖ Pen
- ❖ Journal

What not to take or do in the secret place?

- ❖ Cell Phone
- ❖ Talk on the phone
- ❖ Have the television on

What do you do in the secret place?

- ❖ Praise Him by being thankful and grateful
- ❖ Worship Him for who He is
- ❖ Love on Him and tell Him how great He is
- ❖ Read your Bible
- ❖ Pray and talk to Him through your prayers *(Moses talked face to face with God as a man would talk to his friend)*
- ❖ Pray for your life, your family, friends, and those in authority
- ❖ Pray to the Father in the Name of Jesus

- ❖ Be quiet before Him – Give Him an opportunity to speak to your heart
- ❖ Write down what you receive into your heart in your journal
- ❖ Reinforce who you are by saying positive things about yourself

When you purposefully put into practice the above steps, your relationship with God will grow and develop to such a place of intimacy that you will find your "Sweet Spot". You will come to a place of oneness in your relationship, when you know that you are loved by Him. It's a place of such intimacy that you *"want"* to spend time there. You will know that you are His and He is yours. You are in the *Sweet Spot*.

More Wisdom....

The book of Psalms, Proverbs and/or the book of St. John are great places to start reading your Bible for developing or strengthening your relationship. The book of Psalms is also known as the Book of Praises. This book explores a full range of life's experiences in a very personal and practical way. Almost every Psalm contains a note of praise to God. The book of Proverbs is a book on everyday wisdom; the ability to live life skillfully. This book will help you to make the right decisions and choices in everyday situations. The book of St. John will help you to get to know about Jesus Christ as your Savior. The entire Bible is one you will want to eventually read through as you grow and develop. Decide in your heart now that you will love God with all of your heart, all of your soul, and all of your might.

I have included a sample Daily Devotional as a reference for you as your relationship develops.

30 Days of Wisdom and Virtue

Day 1 Proverbs 1 Psalm 1, 31, 61, 91, 121 John 1:1-28	Day 2 Proverbs 2 Psalm 2, 32, 62, 92, 122 John 1:29-2:1-6	Day 3 Proverbs 3 Psalm 3, 33, 63, 93, 123 John 2:7-3:10	Day 4 Proverbs 4 Psalm 4, 34, 64, 94, 124 John 3:11-4:1-3	Day 5 Proverbs 5 Psalm 5, 35, 65, 95, 125 John 4:4-32	Day 6 Proverbs 6 Psalm 6, 36, 66, 96, 126 John 4:33-5:7	Day 7 Proverbs 7 Psalm 7, 37, 67, 97, 127 John 5:8-36
Day 8 Proverbs 8 Psalm 8, 38, 68, 98, 128 John 5:37-6:18	Day 9 Proverbs 9 Psalm 9, 39, 69, 99, 129 John 6:19-47	Day 10 Proverbs 10 Psalm 10, 40, 70, 100, 130 John 6:48-7:13	Day 11 Proverbs 11 Psalm 11, 41, 71, 101, 131 John 7:14-44	Day 12 Proverbs 12 Psalm 12, 42, 72, 102, 132 John 7:45-8:21	Day 13 Proverbs 13 Psalm 13, 43, 73, 103, 133 John 8:22-51	Day 14 Proverbs 14 Psalm 14, 44, 74, 104, 134 John 8:52-9:21
Day 15 Proverbs 15 Psalm 15, 45, 75, 105, 135 John 9:22-10:9	Day 16 Proverbs 16 Psalm 16, 46, 76, 106, 136 John 10:10-38	Day 17 Proverbs 17 Psalm 17, 47, 77, 107, 137 John 10:39-11:25	Day 18 Proverbs 18 Psalm 18, 48, 78, 108, 138 John 11:26-57	Day 19 Proverbs 19 Psalm 19, 49, 79, 109, 139 John 12:1-28	Day 20 Proverbs 20 Psalm 20, 50, 80, 110, 140 John 12:29-13:7	Day 21 Proverbs 21 Psalm 21, 51, 81, 111, 141 John 13:8-35
Day 22 Proverbs 22 Psalm 22, 52, 82, 112, 142 John 13:36-14:21	Day 23 Proverbs 23 Psalm 23, 53, 83, 113, 143 John 14:22-15:14	Day 24 Proverbs 24 Psalm 24, 54, 84, 114, 144 John 15:15-27	Day 25 Proverbs 25 Psalm 25, 55, 85, 115, 145 John 16:1-20	Day 26 Proverbs 26 Psalm 26, 56, 86, 116, 146 John 16:21-17:16	Day 27 Proverbs 27 Psalm 27, 57, 87, 117, 147 John 17:17-18:19	Day 28 Proverbs 28 Psalm 28, 58, 88, 118, 148 John 18:20-19:8
Day 29 Proverbs 29 Psalm 29, 59, 89, 149 John 19:9-37	Day 30 Proverbs 30 Psalm 30, 60, 90, 120, 150 John 19:38-20:23	Day 31 Proverbs 31 Psalm 119 John 20:24-21:25				

30 Days of Wisdom and Virtue

Begin on Day 1 – and for each day after you will read the scriptures for that day. As you are growing and developing read only what you can for that day and do the same thing each day thereafter. The most important thing is not how much you read but that you develop a pattern of reading your Bible daily.

How Do You Pray?

As we grow older, and the more we stay in the Word, the more our prayers should mature. Building good prayer habits are essential in the walk of a born again Christian. Did you know that Jesus gave us the blueprint on how to pray? Check it out in The Gospel according to Matthew chapter 6. When we are in an attitude of prayer, we are actually approaching the throne of God and communing with The Father through His Son Jesus Christ. As a QNT, we should develop our prayer life and practices. How do we begin developing a prayer life-style?

- ❖ Choose a specific place to pray, away from distractions. (sounds familiar?…Yes, it's your secret place)
- ❖ Attempt to pray at the same time every day. This is how habits are formed
- ❖ Pray out Loud. Hearing yourself talk to God forces you to concentrate on what you are praying about
- ❖ Keep your journal and pen handy. Sometimes through prayer, God reveals things to us. You will want to keep notes of these revelations
- ❖ Pray scripture. Pray God's Word back to Him

Did you know that you can have what you say if you believe it in your heart?

You sure can... Job 22:28 reads *"You will also declare a thing, and it will be established for you; So light will shine on your ways."* As a QNT you want to begin saying positive uplifting biblical things about yourself because your words are powerful!

Affirmations for QNT's

As a QNT you will want to only say (confess) about yourself what God says about you. This will help you to have the self-esteem that comes from God's Word, which is lasting...

I am fearfully and wonderfully made - Psalm 139:14

I am loved by God - Ephesians 3:16-20

I am the apple of God's eye - Psalm 17

I am created for God's Glory - Isaiah 43:7

I am God's trophy - Ephesians 2:10

I am complete in Christ - Colossians 2:10

I have perfect peace because I keep my mind on the Lord – Isaiah 26:3

I am protected and kept safe by the blood of Jesus - Psalm 91

I have friends of like precious faith - Proverbs 27:17

I am whole, Spirit, Soul and in my Body - 1 Thessalonians 5:23

I tithe and I am a giver and it is given back to me - Malachi 3:10-11

I am a saver. I am good at saving money - 3 John 1:2

I am a good steward over the money that I receive - Psalm 25:12-13

I am a good student; learning comes easy to me - 1 Corinthians 2:16

I delight in the Lord and He gives me the desires of my heart - Psalm 37:4

I am patient, I am kind, and I am full of joy - Galatians 5:22-23

I am gentle, I am humble, and I have self-control – Galatians 5:22-23

I am teachable – Matthew 18:4

I do good to others and it comes back to me – Luke 6:38

I use my faith - Matthew 17:20

I have Godly character – Romans 5:4 NLT

I am a QNT; God's daughter – 1 Peter 2:9

The Virtuous QNT

What is virtue? Virtue is being morally pure and good. God's Word gives us an example of a morally pure and good woman in Proverbs 31. As a QNT, this is an example of God's ultimate desire for you. He desires that you know that godly traits are in you, and as you developing they will SHINE through you.

PROVERBS 31 GODLY TRAITS

PRICELESS
10. Who can find a noble wife? She is worth more than rubies.

TRUSTED
11. Her husband trusts her completely. She gives him all the important things he needs.

GOOD NATURED
12. She brings him good, not harm, all the days of her life.

HARDWORKING
13. She chooses wool and flax, She loves to work with her hands.

INDUSTRIOUS
14. She is like the ships of traders. She brings her food from far away.

PROACTIVE
15. She gets up while it is still dark. She provides food for her family. She also gives some to her female servants.

CONSIDERATE
16. She considers a field and buys it. She uses some of the money she earns to plant a vineyard.

STRONG
17. She gets ready to work hard. Her arms are strong.

DILIGENT
18. She sees that her trading earns a lot of money. Her lamp does not go out at night.

TALENTED
19. With one hand she holds the wool. With the other she spins the thread.

HELPFUL
20. She opens her arms to those who are poor. She reaches out her hands to those who are needy.

NO FEAR/FULL OF FAITH
21. When it snows she's not afraid for her family. All of them are dressed in the finest clothes.

WELL GROOMED
22. She makes her own bed coverings. She is dressed in fine linen and purple clothes.

GOOD REPUTATION
23. Her husband is respected at the city gate. There he takes his seat among the elders of the land.

PRUDENT
24. She makes linen clothes and sells them. She supplies belts to the traders.

HONORABLE
25. She puts on strength and honor as if they were her clothes. She can laugh at the days that are coming.

GRACIOUS
26. She speaks wisely. She teaches faithfully.

ATTENTIVE
27. She watches over family matters. She is busy all the time.

BLESSED
28. Her children stand up and call her blessed. Her husband also rises up, and he praises her.

VIRTUOUS
29. He says, "Many women do noble things. But you are better than all the others."

RESPECTFUL
30. Charm can fool you. Beauty fades. But a woman who has respect for the Lord should be praised.

PROSPEROUS
31. Give her the reward she has earned. Let everything she has done bring praise to her at the gate.

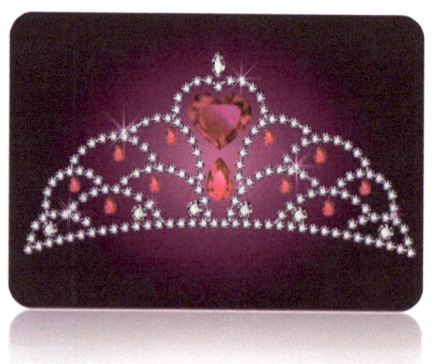

Chapter 2

The Master's Piece

Godly Self-Esteem

Society or culture doesn't define you; Only God defines you!

And God said let us make man in our image after our likeness; Gen 1:26

Godly self-esteem and self-image are important. They are important because you were made in the image and after the likeness of God Himself and you now represent HIM. This is so AMAZING! GOD wants the very best for you and He wants you to make Him proud in everything you do.

While your outward appearance is important, what's most important is your "HEART", and having respect for yourself. The heart that I'm referring to is not the organ that pumps blood, but the part of you that thinks, feels and believes …The Real YOU! When you respect yourself you think properly about yourself. This is having Godly self-esteem, which will be reflected in how you carry yourself. Therefore, never allow yourself or anyone else to make you feel less than God's best.

As you are developing, always remember the traits of the virtuous woman in Proverbs 31 because she respects herself and has good self-esteem. Additionally, I have included an "In Him, In Whom, In Christ" chart with Scriptures to help remind you of whom you are in Christ.

Below is a list of scriptures that you can read and confess daily. These scriptures will help you as you develop your Godly image and self-esteem, and will also serve as a reminder of who you are as an individual! They will help to reinforce who you are in Christ. See yourself through the eyes of God.

N CHRIST	IN HIM	THROUGH CHRIST	WITH CHRIST
I Corinthians 1:21	Acts 17:28	Hebrews 13:20-21	Romans 6:8
I Corinthians 5:17	John 1:4	Galatians 3:13-14	Galatians 2:20
Galatians 3:26-28	John 3:15-16	Galatians 4:7	Ephesians 2:5
Ephesians 1:3	Colossians 2:10	Ephesians 2:7	Colossians 2:20
Ephesians 2:10	I John 5:20	Hebrews 10:10	Colossians 3:1
Philippians 3:13-14	I John 5:14, 15	Hebrews 13:20-21	Colossians 3:3

"Thy Word have I hid in my heart that I might not sin against you" Psalm 119:11

Emotions

"I think myself happy…" Acts 26:2

As a QNT you will experience different types of emotions as during this time-frame they are constantly changing. This is normal because your hormones are beginning to develop. You will notice you may have mood swings, which can affect your attitude. Many times this is due to the start of your menstrual cycle. Mood swings during this time are also known as Pre-Menstrual Syndrome or PMS. Your menstrual cycle will begin sometime during this phase of your life if it hasn't already started. This is normal and to be expected.

Your diet which should include drinking lots of water and being physically fit (active life-style) can help with potential mood swings and PMS, and even sometimes menstrual discomfort.

Learning to manage your emotions may seem difficult to do; however it is necessary and beneficial for all of your relationships as a QNT. Most people don't like being around young ladies who are always moody or who more often than not demonstrate having a bad attitude. Work at having a good attitude and balanced emotions. You do this by intentionally thinking positive thoughts and by deciding to Glorify God with your body, and this includes your attitude. As you remember this, it will help you to have balanced emotions.

Allowing your emotions to have control over you can lead to depression. Christians are meant to be the happiest people on this earth. The following scriptures are good to read out loud whenever you feel your emotions are spinning out of control:

Philippians 4:8
II Corinthians 10:5

Chapter 3

Chasity...

'A Lost Treasure'

The word *chastity* is defined as:
1. The state of being chaste; purity
2. Abstinence from sexual intercourse; virginity or celibacy
3. Sexual morality or abstinence
4. Virtue

The word *treasure* is defined as:
1. Something you hold dear or cherish
2. Something to be valued and appreciated
3. One considered especially precious or valuable
4. Any possession that is highly valued by its owner

Chastity is a treasure that must be re-discovered and highly valued. It is precious before God and should be precious to you! Chastity is not just abstaining from sex until marriage, and that it is, but it is also an understanding that "You" as a QNT are the treasure!

You are the treasure that should not be unlocked or touched until the right time. The right and only time is marriage. Sex is solely reserved for the covenant and commitment of marriage. When you participate in sexual activity, it's not just a physical act, but it is actually giving yourself away. Each time you are sexually active with someone, you are joining (fusing) yourself emotionally to this individual for life. As a QNT, you must value yourself as precious and valuable. You must value yourself to such a degree that you recognize that you are well worth the wait. If you don't value yourself and your self-worth, then nobody else will.

In today's society (the world), being chaste or remaining sexually pure is taboo. It's just not the thing to do, as everyone else is "doing it". However, just because everyone is "doing it" doesn't mean it's the right path. The path of sexual immorality exposes one to:

Sexual diseases
Teenage pregnancy (Being an unwed mother)
Emotional unrest
Potential of making bad choices based on your own personal convictions

Simply stated… it's baggage!
God never intended for you to ever have to experience these things. God has thoughts of peace and good toward you, to give you a wonderful end! His end for you is that you would be found by the man of your dreams and be able to stand knowing that you kept yourself for your wedding night.

Now I know that some of you may feel like you have already messed up in this area. It's Okay. You can start fresh right now. Repent and turn from sexual immorality! Recognize your value and the beauty of chastity. Make a decision from this day forward that you will save yourself until marriage.

QNT remember, you are a Treasure and Well Worth the Wait!

Chapter 4

Stolen Innocence

The thief comes only in order to steal and kill and destroy…
(John 10:10 AMP)

As a QNT it's important to know and understand that there is an enemy out there whose mission is to steal, kill, and destroy God's beloved daughters. One of his tactics is through sexual perverseness, whether through incest, molestation, fondling or rape. These acts are a violation of God's original plan.

If there is someone in your life that had been or is making inappropriate advances towards you, it doesn't matter who they are, they need to be reported to authorities immediately. Please know that you have done nothing wrong. IT'S NOT YOUR FAULT!

This chapter is written to arm you with information you need to be aware of if you or someone you know are in this situation. It's important that you know there are options and resources available to protect you.

Below is some information on molesters and pedophiles:

Molestation is a crime of sexual acts enforced on a person, including touching of private parts, exposure of genitalia, taking of pornographic pictures, rape, induced sexual behavior with the molester or other children. Molestation also applies to incest, which are sexual acts between relatives (close family members).

A pedophile is a molester. The slight difference in definition between a pedophile and a molester has to do with the way the offender gains access to you. Although women can be pedophiles, 80-85% of pedophiles are men. Most pedophiles are close friends, family members, or people who work with youth. They usually have no criminal record and live double lives in an attempt to hide their real motive and not appear obvious to adults. Pedophiles either think that they are as young as you, or you are as old as them. They either don't realize or don't care that they are harming you.

Beware of extra friendly or charming men who like to frequently touch or hug you in non-sexual ways. Sometimes men who are close to you, people you trust because of their title, position or family ties can betray you.

A pedophile can challenge your boundaries by introducing physical contact that is non-sexual in nature initially. Eventually it leads to sex talk, dirty jokes, fondling and inappropriate touching then sex.

A pedophile is a predator. He will take you places; give you gifts and money and display love and affection to win your trust. But his motive is to eventually have sexual relations.

Sexual abuse exists in a relationship when there is unequal power and sexual behavior that is abusive or prohibited by law. An adult having sexual relations with a minor is prohibited by law.

Fondling, oral sex (simulated or actual), intercourse, exhibitionism, taking sexually explicit pictures of youth, showing sexually explicit material to youth or having sex in front of a youth are all considered child sexual abuse.

Although I have never personally experienced any of the above situations, my heart in writing this is to equip you with knowledge and information as to what to be alerted to. If you have faced any of the above situations, you are not alone. Several people have gone through some type of sexual abuse and were threatened not to tell or convinced not to report the matter to law enforcement. GET HELP! Go to your local authorities.

There are things we experience in life that God never meant for us to experience. Although situations such as these are devastating, God WILL help you get through it. God has a master plan for you that cannot be stopped by past experiences. God loves YOU. You are the apple of His eye! (Psalm 17:8). God's desire is that you have healthy, pure relationships. Please understand that you are **not** guilty; you are loved by GOD.

Statistics state that one-third of pregnant teenagers will have an abortion. An abortion is the deliberate termination of a human pregnancy. Although abortion is legal, as a QNT, you must realize that abortion is wrong and it is a sin according to God's Word. There are so many reasons that teenagers have abortions, however no reason should ever justify the killing of a human.

As a QNT you must realize that just as you have been chosen by God, the baby resulting from unprotected sex or even from a tragic situation like "rape" has been chosen as well. What many fail to see when faced with the decision of having the baby or having an abortion is that God has an ultimate purpose in mind for that child. Jeremiah 1:5 says, *"Before I formed thee in the belly I knew thee; and before thou camest forth out of the womb I sanctified thee, and I ordained thee a prophet unto the nations."* As a QNT, understand that the decision to terminate a pregnancy is a decision to end someone's life and their potential for greatness. Know that there are alternatives to abortion, such as, trusting God to raise the child yourself or even adoption.

As a QNT you don't want to live with the regret and guilt of ending a child's life. The guilt and regret can go on for years after the decision has been made. I say to you, choose life and give the child the same opportunity that you were given.

Now, if you are a QNT and have had an abortion, ask for God's forgiveness. God is merciful and just. He is full of compassion and He will forgive you. Don't allow your past decision to plague you for the rest of your life. In addition, you must also forgive yourself.

Decide from this day forward that:

1) You won't engage in pre-marital sex as it is wrong before God
2) You will never ever yield to the world's quick fix to an unplanned pregnancy, "abortion".

Beloved, this is the story of my birth as told by my Mom:

15 and Pregnant

When I think about how naïve I was at 15, I think about you QNT and your innocence. My desire for you is that you enjoy your youth. I want so much for you to remain pure, honoring your bodies as a living sacrifice to God, as stated in Romans 12:4.

I can easily remember the day I was playing with some friends in the basement of my girlfriend's house. We were laughing, talking and playing games. A couple of the girls were off to the side talking about boys. My curiosity got the best of me and I wanted to know exactly what they were saying. As I came to find out, they were talking about "doing it". My girlfriend was talking about how good it was. She spoke of lightning bolts and fireworks that she saw, and the great feelings that she had. Oh, she made it sound so exciting! She talked about kissing and the tingles that you feel in your body. We laughed and giggled. She made us promise not to tell anybody she was "doing it". It was our little secret.

We had fun with the boys in our class. We played and talked with them a lot. A couple of them liked me, but they were more like brothers than anything else. We would run and see who could run the fastest and we'd also play basketball together. Sometimes they would touch me in an inappropriate way and I'd yell and threaten them, they would apologize and that would be the end of that.

Then along came a boy named Larry who was a little older than me. He was so cute. He dressed nice and lived on the other end of the city. I never really had anyone pay attention to me the way he did. The other boys that liked me would pull my hair, hit me, and just do the stupid things boys that age did. But Larry was different. He was more mature than my classmates. I remember when I would see him in school he would leave the guys he was walking up the hallway with and come and say something to me and then run and catch back up with his buddies. I felt so special. My girlfriends would tease me about him. He played football after school. But sometimes he would just show up at my house. We would talk on the phone for hours. My girlfriends would tease me saying go on and give him some.

One night as I was babysitting, I invited him over. We were kissing and one thing led to another and we "did it". It was very painful. I didn't see the fireworks or lightning bolts that my girlfriend had spoken of. None of the glamour that she shared with us was there. It was just painful and messy. He left saying he would call me tomorrow. I remember there being blood on the sheet. I had to clean up the mess that I had made. The next day the lady that I baby sat for was asking me about the sheet as she thought I had my cycle.

After that, I continued to go on about my life as if nothing had happened. He and I didn't talk about what we did much. We both just went on as if nothing had happened. He would still come by and we would talk, but it was different from the way it was before. Things seemed more intense. I really didn't care because I was the captain of the cheerleading team, I was popular and in the tenth grade, and was having fun.

I noticed that my body began to change. I still had my cycle each month. My breasts started getting bigger and they were sore. My Mom took me to the doctor for a pregnancy test and it came back negative. I remember going to the doctor a few times during this six month period. Other than my breasts being heavy, I was fine.

Then it happened. I was doing a split at our school's basketball game and couldn't get back up. The basketball team was coming back on the floor and I was still in my split stance. My cheering squad had to come and help me up. I jumped around more and started bleeding heavily. I went home in so much pain. My stomach was cramping and I felt like I had to have a bowel movement. I was going back and forth to the bathroom. I was in my Mom and Dad's round bed because it was closer to the bathroom and I kept going back and forth. Around six o'clock in the morning, my Auntie Annie Ruth from around the corner and my mom's friend Mrs. Nelson from around the other corner came over and were hovering over me.

They were asking me if I had ever had sex, I told them "no". They told me that I needed to tell the truth, I swore to them that I was telling the truth. The baby's head was coming out and they were telling me that I did "something". I was in pain yelling "take it out", "get it out of me", "it's hurting me". I delivered around 7:15 am and was rushed to the hospital. When I arrived at the hospital, still not knowing exactly what was going on, I found out that we both almost died that day. The placenta was still inside of me and attached to the baby that lay along side of me. I remember seeing her and she was so small she could fit in the palm of my hand.

That evening my Mom was there at the hospital talking to me. She was sitting in the chair and asked me why I didn't tell her the truth that I had sex. I still denied that I had sex. She told me that I had to have had sex because I had a baby. I remembered looking at her like she was stupid and I asked her what was sex. Actually, I had never heard of that terminology; my girlfriends had never mentioned that word. The look on her face saddened me because she never discussed "sex" with me. I could remember hearing my Dad saying "yawl better keep your dresses down" or "don't bring no babies up in here". I heard the words, but never really thought about it.

As we continued to talk, I told her about the time when Larry and I had "did it". But I didn't think that it counted because I was supposed to see "fireworks and lightning bolts" like my girlfriends had told me about and I didn't, so I didn't think about it anymore. My Mom got up from that chair and held me so tight and tears were in her eyes running down her cheeks. She apologized to me for not telling me about "sex". She told me that she loved me and that she was here for me. Even though I knew that she and my Dad loved me, those words were never spoken in our household, but I never felt more loved than I felt at that very moment.

Nonstop we continued to talk. She asked if I wanted to marry Larry. I said no, I didn't want to trap him. I told her I was sorry and I felt so stupid for listening to my friends. I wanted to give the baby up for adoption. I was only 15. I was too young! Plus I didn't want my Dad to be mad at me. My Dad was expecting me to go to the Olympics. She listened, but she gently changed my mind. She told me that my baby was born with a "halo" over her head and that means God has something good in store for her. I still didn't care. I thought my life was over. Momma went on to tell me that my oldest sister had bought clothes for her and that she wanted to name her Stephanie Denise. Mom also said that Mrs. Nelson told her that she would keep the baby for me while I finished school. It seemed that they had made all the decisions for me. At that moment my life was changed forever. My childhood was over, I had to grow up and face responsibilities.

Momma said everything would be fine. Through it all, it all did work out fine. I went through the struggles of raising a child alone. Everything changed - of course my relationship with my Dad changed. I was no longer his little track star…all the awards and ribbons that I had, no longer held the same meaning anymore. I had a stigma of sorts; the girls that I thought were my friends, no longer were. We didn't have the same things in common anymore. I felt like I was tarnished because I had a baby. The boys were only coming around me because that thought that I was "putting out". As I got older, I found guys didn't want to get serious with me because they didn't want to date someone with a kid.

But I was blessed. I was able to continue my education after high school. I held good positions at my jobs and was able to put her in the better schools. Of course I made plenty of mistakes along the way but God was there to help me through. I always wanted her to have more than I had and not experience the things that I had experienced. I did the best that I could.

I needed to share these things with you because they are real and they actually happened. I was young and naïve. I listened to what my girlfriends had to say. I believed them. I didn't know any better. It was a lot of peer pressure.

But you stand a chance! I didn't receive the teachings from home or at church that you may now be privileged to receive. Take heed to the things that you are being taught. I'm asking you to trust in what the Word says, believe in Him! He is a just God. Listen to the wise authority figures in your lives. Through the grace of God, I have a beautiful daughter that is fulfilling the calling that God has on her life. Just take heed to the scripture of the Proverbs 31 woman. The woman to be admired and praised is the woman who lives in the Fear-of-God.

In Love, Ma Deb

My mom's story is one of stolen innocence because she wasn't taught and didn't know what "sex" was and that sex and "doing it" are the same thing. Her story was included to expose one of the many ways the enemy tries to steal, kill, and destroy. It also exposes the importance of having the "right" friends and the importance of parents talking to their children about difficult topics. If you have a friend or friends who are encouraging you to have sex or to "do it", you should see them as an agent of the "enemy" who is trying to steal, kill and destroy your life. Once again, sex is to be reserved for the covenant of marriage between a man and a woman. I Corinthians 6:18 says "Flee Fornication"... Fornication is sex outside of marriage. God is saying basically to run for your life regarding sex outside of marriage. He is very clear about this as any loving Father would be. Although God's mercy and grace got us through those times, life was much more difficult for us than it needed to be; actually it was "hard" and a "real struggle". We want you to intentionally have a blessed life by keeping yourself until you say, "I do".

Stef (right) and me (left) at a Hat and Tea Extravaganza

Chapter 5

Sexy or Beautiful? That is the question...

 Vs

Modesty

...adorn themselves in modest apparel. 2 Timothy 2:9

Modesty is the way we honor God in our outward appearance. We are fearfully and wonderfully made (Psalm 139:14). Our bodies are God's prized possession so it matters how we care for our bodies.

Modesty is defined as a state of being modest, which is behaving, dressing, speaking in a way that is proper or decent.

Beauty comes from the inside out. Being beautiful has to do with character and virtue, and the qualities that make a person who they are.

Sexy is carnal and fleshy. It is defined as exciting or intended to excite sexual desire. Being sexy has to do with how you dress and how you present yourself.

Being cute is necessary for a QNT. To be cute means to be pretty or attractive especially in a lively, wholesome or dainty way.

As a young lady and a QNT, it's going to be important that you select the right type of clothing.

BEAUTIFUL	**SEXY**
Feminine attitude	Seductive attitude
Complimentary clothing	Revealing clothing
Complement your shape; loose	Tight fitting

As a QNT you must understand that how you dress can and will determine how you are addressed. Your attire will either command respect or disrespect.

A Few Tips on Modesty

- Your clothing should be clean and neat
- Your clothing should cover your precious body and never reveal private parts
- Your clothing should complement your shape, but be loose enough to show that you are a lady
- Nails and toes should be well groomed and manicured
- If nail polish is worn, it should be fully on. Chipped polish is not attractive
- Shoes should be neat and polished
- If wearing open toed shoes or sandals, lotion your feet and heels
- Tights or stockings should match your shoes, unless you are wearing skin colored stockings
- Hair styles should complement your image

Body shapes for all QNTs are different based on your culture and background. This means that all clothing does not fit equally. Be mindful when making your selections based on how you are shaped. What's most important is that you are neat, well groomed and that your attire complements your shape. Make clothing selections that complements your image as a QNT. It's your winning attitude, character, personality and disposition that make you beautiful.

QNTs do not dress to get attention. Being sexy is to be luring and captivating. Styles change and seasons change. What is universal is neat attire that is complementary to your shape.

Tattoos

For ye are bought with a price: therefore glorify God in your body, and in your spirit, which are God's.
1 Corinthians 6:20 (KJV)

Tattoos are very popular in today's culture. While popular, marking up the body is not the best display of excellence. Your body is the temple of God. I Corinthians 6:19 (Amp) reads…*Do you not know that your body is the temple (the very sanctuary) of the Holy Spirit Who lives within you, whom you have received [as a Gift] from God? You are not your own..*

Tattoos are permanent markings on the skin; they can also be likened to graffiti, which is commonly seen on buildings. Graffiti diminishes the excellence of buildings as tattoos can diminish the excellence of your physical body and hinder opportunities in your life. Scripture is very clear about tattoos. Leviticus 19:28 (Amp.) reads… *You shall not make any cuttings in your flesh for the dead nor print or tattoo any marks upon you; I am the Lord.*

Body Piercings

Body piercings are also very trendy and popular in today's culture. As a QNT you should never fall into the trap of following the trends and pursuing popularity of the world. Statistics show that most often people get body piercings because they see everyone else doing it. This cannot be your reasoning as a QNT. Just because everyone else is doing it, doesn't mean you should. You are called to be a leader and not a follower!

In addition, as a QNT you must always keep in mind that your body is not yours. Your body is the temple of God! You have been bought with a very high price, the blood of Jesus. Because of this, you should not take it upon yourself to mark or cut your body in any way that would cause the world to question your profession of faith.

Hygiene

Wash thyself therefore, and anoint thee, and put thy raiment upon thee… Ruth 3:3

As a QNT, it is important that we keep our bodies clean. In this section we will cover basic hygiene that will always keep you healthy and fresh.

You should always take a bath or shower every day.

Brush your teeth at least 3 times a day or after every meal.

During your menstrual cycle make sure you stay extra fresh. Shower at night and again in the morning. Use a feminine body freshener. You can purchase them at any grocery or convenience store.

Change your feminine product often and remember to dispose of it properly

Shave excess body hair

Change your underwear everyday (always place dirty clothes in a hamper or designated area in your home). It is unsanitary to have dirty clothes lying around on the floor.

Rinse your washcloth thoroughly so it is free from dirt and soap. After wringing excess water from your washcloth, hang it up to allow it to air dry. Change your washcloth and towel at least once a week or more often as needed.

Wearing Perfume

Here are a few tips on wearing perfume:

- ❖ Always put perfume on your skin and never on your face or on your clothes.
- ❖ Put perfume on your pulse points which are behind your ears, on your wrist, at the bend of your arm, and the back of your legs.
- ❖ Perfume should not be used in place of deodorant.

Hair Care for the QNT

*But the very **hairs** of your head are all numbered. Matthew 10:30*

As a QNT, your hair is a glory to you; therefore it is important that it is cared for and well maintained.

If you are a young QNT, this is done for you. Included below are tips for you to care for your hair as you mature.

Healthy hair starts with a healthy body and lifestyle

Brush and/or comb your hair daily (this will keep it free from tangling and breakage)

Wash your hair regularly – how often depends on your lifestyle and hair texture.

Develop a hair care regimen that works best for you whether you are exercising, bathing, showering or sleeping.

Hair that gets oily quickly may need to be shampooed every other day. Hair that is curly or coarse may need to be shampooed less often, once a week or even once every two weeks. Excessive washing will cause the natural oils in your hair to dry out and cause dullness and breakage.

Due to frequent use of blow dryers and irons, it may be necessary to replace these natural oils with moisturizers, hair oils and other nourishing products.

Blow drying your hair when wet can also be damaging because wet hair is more vulnerable to breakage and split ends.

Drying, straightening or curling hair may cause damage to your hair. Avoid using these hair utensils as your daily regimen. Keep ends trimmed as needed. (See a Professional Stylist for trimming)

While popular and convenient, use perms with caution, as they have been known to damage hair and hair follicles (See a Professional Stylist.)

AQNT's Guide to a Healthy Lifestyle

Who satisfieth thy mouth with good things; so that thy youth is renewed like the eagles. Psalms 103:5

A healthy active lifestyle is vitally important to having a long full life. Here are some tips to help you to be active and healthy:

Drink half of your body weight in water every day

Be active or exercise for at least 30 minutes a day

Eat lots of fruits and vegetables

Take a multi-vitamin (ask your parent or guardian)

Eat a good breakfast, sensible lunch and dinner

Snack on healthy foods as needed

Remember to watch your serving sizes and do not over eat

Suggestions for being active:

Brisk Walks	Jogging	Tennis	Swimming
Ballet	Basketball	Bowling	Soccer
Volleyball	Baseball	Bike Riding	Jump Rope
Gymnastics	Badminton	Racquetball	Squash
Horseback Riding	Cheerleading	Run Track	Karate
Skating	Indoor Rock Climbing		

Chapter 6
Relationships

Obedience, Honor, and Respect

Children, obey your parents in the Lord, for this is right. "Honor your father and mother," which is the first commandment with promise: "that it may be well with you and you may live long on the earth." Ephesians 6:1-3

As a QNT, it is important that you understand that honoring your parents is not an option. Ephesians 6:1-3 reads, "Children obey your parents in the Lord for this is right. Honor your father and mother, which is the first commandment with promise: that it may be well with you and you may live long on the earth." Webster's 1828 dictionary defines "honor" as:

to revere; to respect; to treat with deference and submission.

Honor is not based upon your feelings; it's settled as a commandment from God.

The Adopted QNT

Psalm 27:10 When my father and my mother forsake me, then the LORD will take me up.

In today's society, adoption has become common place. However, those who are a product of adoption often have issues of insecurity, abandonment and low self-esteem. If you are an adopted QNT, you must realize that being adopted does not make you any less than someone who has been raised by their biological parent(s). Do not accept the feelings of insecurity, low self-esteem or abandonment. While it does stand true that your biological parent(s) could not take care of you for any number of reasons, God still had you in the palm of His hands. He is and will always be Your Heavenly Father. He didn't abandon you and He never will!

As an adopted QNT, realize how unique and special you are and how awesome it is to be adopted. Realize that your adoptive parent(s) had a choice and they chose to bring you home. You are special, handpicked and chosen first by God and second by the parent(s) who are raising you. Don't allow the questions of why, what, and how come "my so called real parents" gave me up, torment you. You may never have all the answers. However, the one answer that will always remain is that you are loved by God. As an adopted QNT, be grateful for the parent(s) that God has placed you with. Understand that He cared so much that He would place you with them. Live everyday with the realization of your uniqueness and become a testimony to others of what God can do.

Communication for the QNT

Don't let anyone think less of you because you are young. Be an example to all believers in what you say, in the way you live, in your love, your faith and your purity. 1 Timothy 4:12 (NLT)

As a QNT what you say, and how you say it is vitally important to being successful in life. Below are some tips for you to excel in good communication:

You should always be mindful of your tone. Young ladies should never be heard before they are seen.

When communicating with someone, you should look at them directly in their eyes while you're standing up straight. It's been said that body language is 80% of communication. Have you ever noticed when someone is tired of hearing someone talk? How do you know they are tired of listening to someone talk? You can see it by their physical demeanor. As a QNT, you should always be conscious of your body language.

Remember to give a firm hand shake when meeting or greeting people.

Listen before you speak. Listening is an art which requires your undivided attention. It's always good to write down any questions that may run across your mind while the person is talking. Then wait to ask them your questions after they are done speaking. A lot of times if you allow them to complete what they are communicating to you, they may answer the question(s) that you wrote down to ask them.

Think before you speak. It's always best for a QNT to speak slowly and thoroughly. This may require you to think about what you want to say before saying it.

Build your vocabulary. You can do this by simply picking up the dictionary, and committing to learn a new word every day. If you can use the word in a sentence that day, this will help your memory will store it for future use.

Remember these are just a few tips that will help you on your journey to becoming a great communicator!

QNT and Siblings

As a QNT, it is important to value and appreciate your older and younger siblings. You have a responsibility to love them the way Christ loves you. Your relationship with your siblings should reflect the nature of Christ. When people see you and your sibling(s), they should be able to see the love of God.

It doesn't matter whether you are the older or younger sibling. As a QNT, you have certain responsibilities in your relationship with them.

If you are the older sibling, here are a few of your responsibilities:

1. You should always be mindful that you are an example to your younger sibling. Your younger sibling will most likely do what they see you do. Make sure your lifestyle is one that they can follow.

2. You should always protect them. As much as lies within you, you should make sure that your younger sibling(s) are never harmed.

3. You should spend time with your younger sibling(s) on purpose. Spending time with them means so much in their minds. God is pleased when you do this!

If you are the younger sibling, here are a few of your responsibilities:

1. You should listen to your older sibling(s), recognizing that they have already been where you are trying to go.

2. You should be respectful of your older sibling's things such as their clothing, jewelry, etc. You shouldn't take it upon yourself to borrow something without asking.

3. You should spend time with your older sibling(s). Count it as a great joy to spend quality time with them.

The QNT and Friendships

A man who has friends must himself be friendly… Proverbs 18:24a, (NKJV)

As a QNT, it is very important that you choose your friends wisely; as your friendships will either make or break you! The friends you hang with today will determine how high you will be able to fly in life.

As this is the case, when selecting friends, you should select friends who are thinking, believing and doing the same things that you are doing. It is very easy to get dragged down by someone who you call a friend that is doing the complete opposite of what you are trying to do. Remember that evil associations corrupt good manners (1 Corinthians 15:33). You want to associate and develop friendships with people whose associations aren't considered evil. Evil associations would be with people who like to gossip, put others down, steal, go clubbing, etc. You don't want to associate with these types of people. In addition, it is important that you know how to be a good friend. Being a good friend ensures that you will always have a good friend. A good friend is loyal, friendly, considerate and selfless. She cares more for her friend than she does herself.

As a QNT, it's also important that you know how to conduct a friendship with the opposite sex. It is okay to have good guy friends but you should steer clear from being labeled one who only has guy friends. You should have a healthy balance of both guy and girl friends. In addition, you want to understand that entertaining anything other than a friendship with a guy at this point in life is not realistic. If you are not old enough to consider marriage, then dating is not for you. As a QNT, you must realize that dating is not about hooking up with the opposite sex because you like them and they like you. Rather, dating is designed for adults when they are preparing for marriage.

Lastly, when it comes to relating to guys, it is never acceptable for you as a QNT to pursue the guy. If you are pursuing a guy, it means that you are asking for his number. It means that you don't wait for the guy to call you, but you engage in excessively calling him or texting him. It also means that you are always in his face. You don't give the guy any breathing room. QNT, remember your value and worth and be mindful that God's plan is that you present yourself as a woman of virtue and allow the guy to pursue and find you. Proverbs 18:22 says, *"Whosoever findeth a wife findeth a good thing and obtained favor of the Lord"*. Let him find you.

As a QNT, do not entertain the idea of having a romantic or sexual relationship with the same sex. A QNT, as previously stated, knows it is healthy to have <u>friendships</u> with other girls. However, it is un-healthy and forbidden according to God's Word, to be romantically involved with someone of the same sex. Romans 1:21 states, *"Because that, when they knew God, they glorified him not as God, neither were thankful; but became vain in their imaginations, and their foolish heart was darkened."*

As a QNT, do not entertain the idea of having a romantic or sexual relationship with the same sex. A QNT, as previously stated, knows it is healthy to have <u>friendships</u> with other girls. However, it is un-healthy and forbidden according to God's Word, to be romantically involved with someone of the same sex. Romans 1:21 states that, "Because that, when they knew God, they glorified him not as God, neither were thankful; but became vain in their imaginations, and their foolish heart was darkened." A QNT does not entertain thoughts of "liking" another girl or "doing it" or "having sex" with another girl or even "marrying" another girl. As a QNT, do not believe "the lie" of the enemy that you were born this way or it is Okay to feel this way. This is deception at its best.

You must quickly get rid of thoughts of being with another girl by doing the following:

1.) **Casting them down** *(2nd Corinthians 10:5, Casting down imaginations, and every high thing that exalts itself against the knowledge of God, and bringing into captivity every thought to the obedience of Christ.)*
2.) **Renew your mind by reading the Word** *(Romans 12:2, And be not conformed to this world: but be ye transformed by the renewing of your mind, that ye may prove what is that good, and acceptable, and perfect, will of God.)*
3.) **Avoid people, places or things that would feed that thought process** *(1st Corinthians 15:33, Be not deceived: evil communications corrupt good manners.)*
4.) **Guard your heart** *(Proverbs 4:23, Keep thy heart with all diligence; for out of it are the issues of life.)*

Ideas like the above come from:

- What you are watching and what you see (eyes)
- Music you are hearing (ears)
- What you are saying with your lips (mouth)
- Who is touching you (hands)

Know this; if you have experimented with the same sex, there is forgiveness in God for you. (*1st John, If we confess our sins, he is faithful and just to forgive us our sins, and to cleanse us from all unrighteousness.*)

Peer Pressure and the QNT

Romans 12:2 Be not conformed to this world….

Peer Pressure is very real in today's society. It is a reality that everyone will encounter. It is real in my life as well as in yours. As a QNT, you must learn to deal with peer pressure or peer pressure will deal with you. Peer pressure will cause you to act and do things outside the boundaries of what you know to be right and wrong.

Peer pressure is defined as social pressure by members of one's peer group to take a certain action, adopt certain values, or otherwise conform in order to be accepted.

As a QNT, you must decide before-hand that you will not conform. You <u>must</u> establish beforehand a set of beliefs and convictions from the basis of God's Word that you will stand true to. It has been said that if you don't stand for something, you will fall for anything. The beliefs and convictions that you establish beforehand will become your foundation and will cause you to stand against the pressure of following the crowd. You will be able to stand, when everyone around you is saying no.

As a QNT, it is truly Okay to be different. Remember you are fearfully and wonderfully made. You are unique and distinguished. You were never made to fit in, but born to stand out for the glory of God! Don't ever allow the approval of any man, woman, boy or girl dictate your actions. You must live for the audience of one, Jesus Christ. Don't allow your peers to put the pressure on you, but you put the pressure back on them by living a life becoming of a Christian and the QNT you were created to be.

A QNT Doesn't Do Drugs

"For ye are bought with a price: therefore glorify God in your body and in your spirit which are God's." 1 Corinthians 6:20

As a QNT you must avoid the common trap of getting entangled with drugs and alcohol of any sort. There's a saying "curiosity killed the cat". As a QNT, don't allow the peer pressure of society around you or the allure of trying something new to cause you to do something you will later regret. Statistics have shown that adult alcoholics and drug addicts can be traced back to their teenage years. As a QNT, you must avoid this at all cost, as statistics have also shown that substance abuse has detrimental effects on your body. Below are just a few of these effects:

ALCOHOL	**TOBACCO**	**DRUGS**
Cirrhosis of the liver	*Bad Breath*	*Mental Impairment*
Kidney Failure	*Loss of teeth*	*Cell Degeneration*
Depressed Nervous System	*Lung Cancer*	*Respiratory Failure*

Remember that you are not your own, you were bought with a price. Therefore glorify God in your body. 1 Corinthians 6:20.

As a QNT, you can avoid the trap of substance abuse and glorify God by 1) Having a conviction that drugs and alcohol are not for you; 2) Avoiding people, places and things where substance abuse is prevalent; and 3) Being able to stand alone when necessary, desiring the approval of God above anybody else.

The QNT and Bullying

You have heard that it was said, 'An eye must be put out for an eye. A tooth must be knocked out for a tooth'. But here is what I tell you. Do not fight against an evil person. Suppose someone hits you on your right cheek. Turn your other cheek to him also. Suppose someone takes you to court to get your shirt. Let him have your coat also. Suppose someone forces you to go one mile. Go two miles with him. Matthew 5:38-31 (NIRV)

As a QNT, you should never bully anyone and you should not allow anyone to bully you or anyone you know. Bullying can manifest itself in several ways: Teasing, spreading rumors, writing or texting mean or threatening notes or posts using the Internet and all forms of Social Media which is commonly referred to as CYBERBULLYING.

As a QNT, you must always treat others the way you want to be treated. You should never be exclusive and belittle those who are different from you. You must recognize that God has created everyone differently and accept the unique differences in others. Stay clear of cliques as cliques exclude others and cause others to have feelings of fear, anxiety and inadequacies.

Now, if you have been treating everyone the way you want to be treated and yet someone has been bullying you, here are some keys to help you deal with your situation:

> Don't stay quiet. Tell someone that you trust so that they can help stop the bullying

Stay calm; don't give into the pressure to respond in a way that would cause you to come out of your Christian disposition.

Look for a way to lovingly confront the source of the bullying without an audience. Your confrontation with the source of bullying should be one on one, as your heart for confronting them is reconciliation.

If lovingly confronting them does not result in a "cease fire" then you should talk to an authority figure, which may include law enforcement. Allow them to handle the bullying for you.

Chapter 7

Back To Basics

Your kindness will reward you… Proverbs 11:17a (NLT)

As a QNT, the first impression you make is the one that is most lasting in the mind of the person you are meeting. It is said you have only 'one' chance to make a first impression. So you always want to make a good first impression. In this section we will be discussing:

    Please and Thank You
    Writing Thank You Notes
    Good Sportsmanship and practical Tips for Everyday Living

Please and Thank You

So often, the words "Please" and "Thank You" are overlooked in everyday conversation. Using these words regularly shows kindness, honor, respect and humility. I have a saying and those that are around me know it quite well. The statement is *"No one has to do anything for you"*. What's the point? The point is to always be appreciative and thankful for any kindness, love or generosity shown to you because people didn't have to choose you to be kind towards. It is the same for you QNTs. As I mentioned earlier, when I was a teenager I had a neutral attitude and disposition. I was neither really happy nor sad, but my attitude sometimes could be really bad because I had an entitlement attitude as if somebody owed me something. Always remember to be thankful and grateful for whatever you have because that keeps the door of God's goodness open to flow to you.

Write a Thank You Note

You can write a thank you note to show appreciation for something someone has done for you. Most people like knowing that the kindness they showed towards you was appreciated. Send a thank you note typically within 7 days of receiving a gift or an act of kindness. The thank you note should be genuine and heartfelt, and always hand written.

Good Sportsmanship for a QNT

And if anyone enters competitive games, he is not crowned unless he competes lawfully (fairly, according to the rules laid down). 2 Timothy 2:5 (AMP)

What is good sportsmanship? It means being in a competitive situation and from start to finish, you conduct yourself in a manner that is respectful and honest. You show dignity and style whether you win or lose. If you win, you know how to remain humble. It is not gracious to make others feel ashamed because they were not the crowned champions. If you lose, a good sport is able to demonstrate a pleasant character towards your opponents.

You must have courage to be a good sport. You know it can be easy to poke your mouth out if you lose a game. You have to remember, that is not what God would want you to do when you lose. Always remain willing to congratulate the winner. You can put in more practice and work harder for the next game.

Here are some ways you can show you are a good sport:

Rules

- Play by the rules of the game
- Do not cheat
- Listen to others and remain obedient to the instructions given
- Accept the judgment calls of the officials; that is why they are present
- Do not make a scene over a ruling; this could cause you further penalties

Mental Preparation

- If you make a mistake, forgive yourself and get back in the game
- When a teammate makes a mistake, encourage them to keep trying
- Know what is expected of you and give it your best effort
- Know your sport and be competitive but not argumentative

Attitude

- Win without bragging; lose without pouting
- Do not blame others; take responsibility for your actions
- Remember to share
- No complaining
- If you do not agree with something, talk respectfully to the proper person

Behavior

- Show respect to your teammates and your opponents
- Self-control is essential
- Use appropriate language
- Be polite
- Physical fighting is never an option
- Treat others the way you want to be treated at all times

A QNT Sits Like a Lady

- Approach your chair from the right side of the chair using the left side of your body

- Before you sit, gently use the back of your legs to feel where your chair is

- After you feel your seat with your legs, <u>gently</u> sit down in the center of the chair

- If you are wearing a dress or skirt, smooth your clothes out before sitting down. Never flop down in a chair

- After you sit, take time to straighten your skirt or dress

- Once you are seated, place both knees together, and always keep your legs closed when sitting in a chair

- Once you have placed your knees together, gently cross your ankles, placing one foot behind the other

- Remember to keep your back straight. No Slouching. Keep your chin up, be proud of who you are. You are God's beautiful QNT!

A QNT is a great Houseguest

...And into whatsoever house ye enter, first say, Peace be to this house.
Luke 10:5 (KJV)

A QNT understands that it is a privilege to be invited to stay at someone's home. With that perspective, it requires that you remember to be on your best behavior, which means to be nice and respectful to everyone at all times. Also, keep in mind that we represent our heavenly Father and that he watches over everything we do and say. God's Word tells us to… *Let your gentleness be known to all men. The Lord is at hand. Philippians 4:5 NKJV*

Below are some tips for being a houseguest for an overnight stay or longer:

What to pack for an overnight stay:

- Use a bag that is appropriate for the length of your stay
- Pack Pajamas and a robe
- Pack socks and/or slippers
- Bring a change of underwear
- Pack a sleeping/slumber bag and a pillow
- Pack a toothbrush and toothpaste
- Pack your face cloth and towel
- Pack a hairbrush and/or comb
- Pack deodorant

Modesty Tip for Sleepovers

Pajamas should cover you up and not be revealing or see through. Your bathrobe should be worn at all times; never walk around with just your pajamas on; Upon waking the next day, wash up or shower and get dressed for breakfast. Remember to:

- Bring a gift
- Clean up after yourself
- Be helpful
- Be mindful of your noise level
- Stay in designated areas (don't wander)
- Have fun
- Say thank you upon leaving or write a thank you note

Self-Esteem Tip for Sleepovers

Monitor your feelings, and be mindful to think the best thoughts of everyone in the environment. Something terrific happens when girls get together. Make it a good time and keep the atmosphere positive because friendships and families are ordained of God. If you notice the positive environment beginning to change negatively, you as God's QNT should endeavor to bring back the peace. Never allow the environment to go sour or negative because of one person, and be quick to get everybody reconciled. God expects you to be a peacemaker. Matthew 5:9 says, *"Blessed are the* **peacemakers**: *for they shall be called the children of God."*

Table Settings and Table Manners

Thou preparest a table before me… Psalm 23:5

As a QNT, you will have many opportunities to demonstrate table manners and it helps to know what to do in those situations. You will learn how to set a table, learn which fork to use and other fun manners that go with learning how to set a table.

There are different styles of table settings that are appropriate for different types of meals or gatherings. We will learn about casual table settings, buffet style table settings, and formal table settings.

Causal Table Setting

This table setting is commonly used daily in your home. When you are asked to "set the table" at home, you create a place setting using:

- Plate (goes in the center)
- Napkin (goes to the left of the plate)
- Salad Fork (smaller fork goes next to the napkin- use this one first)
- Dinner Fork (larger fork goes closest to the plate)
- Knife (to the right of the plate)
- Teaspoon (smaller goes next to knife)
- Tablespoon (larger goes next to the teaspoon; and it is also used for soup)
- Glass (goes above silverware on the right side of the plate)

- Bread plate (goes above forks and napkins on the left of the plate)
- A placemat will help in the placement of the above items and it adds beauty to the table setting.

Buffet Style Setting

This type of setting is normally found at larger informal parties or gatherings, picnics, birthday parties, etc. In this type of setting you normally will serve yourself:

- The plates, utensils and napkins are in a stack.
- Pick up a plate and utensils and head for the food to serve yourself.
- Be sure not to overfill your plate with food.
- Although there is a variety of food, you usually will have an opportunity to try another dish or have a second helping.

Formal Table Setting

This table setting is used for formal banquets or fancy restaurants where you are served by waiters. This setting has more utensils than you normally use. Normally in a formal table setting, your waiter will remove the utensils and dishes that you have used before the next course is served.

- When everyone is seated, place your napkin in your lap (the waiter does this for you if you haven't done it)
- Soup is served (use soup spoon or the spoon that is furthest to your right)
- Salad is served (use your salad fork which is the smaller fork)

When using this table setting, begin using your utensils from the outside that will match the part of the meal being served.

Usually the sequence goes like this;

- A cloth napkin is placed in your lap
- Soup is served (use spoon furthest to your right)
- Salad is served (use fork furthest to your left)
- Bread is served to you or passed around the table in a basket. Select your choice of dinner roll, making sure you do not touch any other roll except yours. Place your roll on the bread plate
- Dinner is served (use your dinner fork and knife)
- Dessert is served after your meal and you will use either a fork or spoon depending on type of dessert

Before You Eat

Wash your hands (if needed, go to the bathroom to wash your hands. This will keep you from having to be excused from the table to go to the bathroom)

- Bless your food – whether at home or in public (including the school lunch room), thank the Lord for the food He has blessed you with!
- Place your napkin in your lap (tucking the edges under your legs will help it stay in place)

After You Eat

- Thank the person who prepared the meal, even if it is take-out food (it is always good manners to show appreciation)
- Wipe your mouth using your napkin, not your hand
- Ask permission to be excused and also ask if you may clear the table
- If using paper plates, plastic forks, paper cups and napkins, discard all into the trash basket. Be sure to pour out any liquid remaining in the cup before you throw it away.
- If using dishes, scrape remaining food particles into the trash basket and carefully rinse the dishes before placing them into the dishwasher or wash them by hand in the sink with a liquid dish detergent. If using cloth napkins, ask where the used napkin should be placed
- Using a dampened dish cloth, wipe the dinner table including placemats. Be sure the crumbs do not end up on the floor

- Sweeping the kitchen floor is also a good idea; make sure you get the corners and under the cabinets

Table Manners

When eating a meal or a quick after school snack, basic table manners must always be followed. Here are a few hints:

- Sit up straight and lift the food to your mouth. Do not lower your head to meet your food
- Do not put your elbows on the table
- Chew with your mouth closed (no one wants to see the contents of your mouth when you are eating)
- In order to chew your food well, take small bites or small forkfuls and count to 20 silently to yourself
- Do not talk with food in your mouth. Conversations at the table are priceless and reinforce bonding time with the family. However, wait until you have finished chewing to talk
- Eat using one hand at a time except when using your knife to cut
- If you desire a food item or a condiment that is across the table, ask someone to pass it to you. It is considered rude to reach across someone's plate
- If you have something in your mouth, (for example a piece of bone, etc) remove it from your mouth discreetly using your fork; it is not necessary to make a funny face or speak loudly about the incident
- If a piece of food is stuck in your teeth, do not attempt to remove it at the table. Wait until after the meal to remove

it. If it is painful, excuse yourself and go to the bathroom to remove the item
- When eating at a small table for 2 to 6 people, it is polite to wait until all have been served before you begin to eat (your food will not get cold); any table larger than 6 people, it is okay to begin eating after two or three people have been served (If you wait until all have been served, your food will get cold)
- After you have asked to be excused from the table, be sure to push your chair under the table. (take a quick look to be sure there are no crumbs or pieces of food in your seat; if there are, remove them and ask for something to wipe the seat with; you want to make sure no one sits on food, sauce or grease left by the dropped food items)
- If you have to burp, do it and say excuse me afterwards (either at the table or anytime); although the sounds of burping are different from person to person, you should never laugh after someone burps
- Although you are using proper table manners when eating, it is rude to correct someone at the table if they are not using proper table manners. If it is your sister, brother, cousins or friends, simply share what you have learned after the meal is over so they will not be embarrassed
- Always say "please" and "thank you" when appropriate
- Be patient with yourself; it will take time to learn good table manners, but soon it will be very easy and you will use them without thinking about it

How to Eat Difficult Foods

Here a few quick hints for eating foods that may be challenging.

Spaghetti – You may be given a spoon and fork to use when eating this type of pasta. If so, pick up a few strands of pasta with your fork, place the fork in the well of the spoon and twirl. If no spoon is given, use the curve of your plate.

Tacos – along with tortillas are eaten with your hands. However, if some of the filling spills out, you are to use a fork to eat that part and not your hands.

Sushi – can usually be eaten whole unless the size is too big. If it is too big for you, use a knife and fork to adjust the size.

Cooking for the QNT

… she bringeth her food from afar. Proverbs 31:14b

Cooking is such fun. You get to create and taste many different foods. God gave us all things to enjoy. Did you know that God gave us all of the necessary things we need for eating through nature? He created water to drink, animals for meat and herbs for seasoning. He also created fruits and vegetables to nourish our bodies. Cooking also creates family memories and great traditions. Remember to be safe in the kitchen.

Sometimes you may be asked for your preference in certain foods. This means what foods you like, and what foods you don't like. You should always be able to articulate your preference. Here is some information about chicken that you may or may not know: What is referred to as the white meat of a chicken is the chicken breast and the chicken wing. What is referred to as the dark meat of a chicken, is the chicken leg and the chicken thigh.

BASIC MEASURING GUIDE

1 Tablespoon (Tbsp)	=	3 Teaspoons (tsp)
½ Cup (c)	=	8 Tablespoons (Tbsp)
¼ Cup (c)	=	4 Tablespoon (Tbsp)
1 Gallon (gal)	=	4 Quarts/8 Pints/ or 16 Cups
Pinch	=	Less than 1/8 Teaspoon (tsp)
1 Quart	=	2 Pints/6 Cups
1 Pint	=	2 Cups
1 Pound (lb)	=	16 ounces (oz)
½ Pound	=	8 ounces
¼ Pound	=	4 ounces

One day, it will be your responsibility as a QNT to cook for your family and to make sure your family has balanced nutritious meals.

Until that time comes, I've included a recipe just for you!

Spaghetti and Meat Balls Recipe

This is a simple recipe for you as a QNT. The more you get in the kitchen the easier it will be for you to start cooking more from scratch. Hopefully this recipe will entice you to get in the kitchen more and perfect the art of cooking.

Ingredients

- ☐ 1lb Lean Ground Beef or Turkey
- ☐ 1 onion
- ☐ 1 garlic clove
- ☐ 1 bell pepper
- ☐ 1 box of spaghetti
- ☐ 2 -16oz jars of spaghetti sauce (such as Ragu Garden combination or whatever variety that you like)
- ☐ 1 teaspoon of seasoning salt
- ☐ 1 teaspoon of garlic powder
- ☐ ½ teaspoon of Italian seasoning
- ☐ 2 ½ tablespoons of olive oil

Directions

1. Bring water to a boil and add a pinch of salt, and a teaspoon of olive oil

2. Add spaghetti (COOK ACCORDING TO INSTRUCTIONS ON BOX)

3. Drain spaghetti using a food drainer/strainer

4. Dice/chop bell pepper, onion, and garlic

5. In a heated skillet, add a teaspoon of olive oil, onion, bell pepper, and garlic

Sauté until bell pepper is soft and onion and garlic are clear. Allow mixture to cool

6. Get a bowl and season your meat with seasoning salt, garlic powder, Italian seasoning, and add the onion, bell pepper, and garlic mixture to it. Stir gently to combine the ingredients, or you can use your hands to combine all the ingredients, but make sure you wash them first.

7. Roll mixture into balls – you do this by rolling the mixture in your hands in a circular motion. Then place balls into a heated skillet (on medium) with 2 tablespoons of olive oil cover and cook for 15 minutes or until turkey or beef is well done

8. Put spaghetti back into pot. Add spaghetti sauce and meatballs to pot. Let simmer for 15 minutes.

Chores for the QNT

Let all things be done decently and in order. 1 Corinthians 14:40

Doing chores and being prepared helps you as a QNT to develop into the virtuous young lady that God has called you to be. Remember, you can do all things through Christ which strengthens you.

Below are some chores that you will begin doing:

How to Clean the Sink and Bathtub

> Spray cleaning solution around the entire sink or bathtub
>
> Run water in the bath tub
>
> Using a sponge make circling motions with the sponge, cleaning the ring or dirty areas
>
> Rinse the bath tub or sink with water until the water is clear and sink and tub are clean

How to Clean the Kitchen

Before we begin I must tell you that when you have the duty to clean the kitchen, this does not mean clean the dishes only. Let's first come to the realization that as a QNT you need to clean the entire kitchen. When cleaning the kitchen, it's always proper to first take any leftover food from the meal and put it in the proper container. Store it in the refrigerator for another meal.

Remember QNTs are faithful stewards over everything God blesses them with.

Clean out the food remains from the pots that were used to cook the meal; QNTs aren't lazy therefore they do not hide dirty pots in the stove. After scraping the food remains into the trash, put the pots aside so you can clean them after you've completely washed the dishes. Some pots may require you putting water in them, and boiling them on the stove. This will help you to clean them easier.

When preparing to wash the dishes, you should pour out all liquids that may be left over in the cups first. Next, scrape all leftover food off the plates. Then stack all dishes together…stack all the dirty plates together; stack all the bowls together; put all the cups together; and place all the silverware together. It's important that you clean out the sink before making your dish water, unless you are using a dishwasher.

If you are using a dishwasher, rinse each item thoroughly and place it in the dishwasher accurately. If you are hand washing the dishes, clean the sink out before making your dish water.

It's proper to use hot water when cleaning the dishes. Hot water helps to sterilize and kill germs, so make the dish water as hot as you can stand it. You can also use plastic gloves. Start with the cups, plates, bowls, utensils, and then wash the pots and pans at the end. Make sure you properly rinse each dish. After you've cleaned and rinsed all the dishes, now it's time to get a drying towel, dry them and put them in the proper cabinet for storage.

After you've completed all the above steps, use a small amount of fresh hot dish water to wipe down the kitchen table, refrigerator, countertops, backsplash, microwave and stove top. Then drain the dirty dishwater and clean the sink out.

Now it's time to sweep. When sweeping, make sure you get in the corners really good, and take your time. There is nothing worse than walking on a dirty floor. After sweeping, take the time to mop the floor thoroughly if needed.

How to Mop the Floor

Make sure you get the right cleaning detergent to put in the bucket. As a word of advice, NEVER mix Bleach or Ammonia together as these two agents will cause a dangerous reaction. People have been known to lose consciousness, vomit uncontrollably, or taken to the emergency room for treatment. I recommend you use a cleaning agent specifically designed for floors.

When mopping, you should always mop yourself out of the kitchen; so in order to do this you should start on the other side of the room, the furthest away from the entrance to the kitchen. Then work yourself out of the kitchen. Now you can allow the floor time to dry. While you're allowing the floor time to dry, dispose of the dirty mop water; it's appropriate to dispose of the dirty water into the toilet, or wherever your parent directs you to. After the floor dries, if you need to put the mop back in its proper place, this would be the time to do so.

Now take a moment to look over the kitchen to make sure you didn't leave anything out of place. Remember everything has its proper place.

Good Job QNT!

The Proper Way to Make a Bed

- Pull the flat sheet (sheet on top) across the entire bed
- Make sure it is even and there are no lumps in the sheets
- Tuck the sheet under the mattress
- Repeat this process for your blanket
- Pull your comforter up to the top of the bed as you did for you sheet and blanket
- Place your pillow(s) on top of the comforter or you may pull your comforter over your pillow(s) (This is a personal preference).
- Linen should be changed once a week at a minimum
- Mattress should be rotated semi quarterly

A QNT always keeps her room neat, clean and organized because it gives you peace and a sense of <u>order.</u>

How to wash clothes properly

1. <u>Sort Your Washing</u>
   Sort your washing into four categories; whites, coloreds, delicate fabrics, and heavily soiled. In this way, you'll save your clothes from changing colors and be able to decide which kind of detergent to use. Washing powder that has been developed especially for colored clothes contains no bleach.

2. <u>Use a Laundry Net</u>
   To avoid damaging delicate and fragile items like underwear, wired bras should be washed in a laundry net.

3. <u>Prevent Tearing</u>
   Make sure buttons, hooks and zips are fastened before washing. This prevents them from being ripped off in the machine, or other clothes being torn by them.

4. <u>Check Pockets</u>
   Check all pockets; one single forgotten Kleenex will shred and leave a mess - even worse is a forgotten, leaky pen.

5. <u>Don't Over-load the Washing Machine</u>
   The inside of the washing machine should be full, but not over-loaded. During rotation, the clothes rub together which aids cleaning. Too many clothes will prevent the clothes from moving around in the machine.

6. _Turn Clothes Inside Out_
   Turn your clothes inside out. This keeps their color fresh and stops color fading.

7. _How much Washing Powder?_
   Find out how hard or soft the water in your area is. You'll need to use more washing powder if the water is hard, less if it is soft. (rule of thumb, the water in Florida is considered hard unless you have a water softening system connected to your water supply.)

8. _Keep the Machine Clean and Fresh_
   Close the washing machine door when completed to prevent mildew and mustiness.

9. _Clean the dryer's lint filter after each drying cycle._

How to Thread a Needle and Sew on a Button

"She layeth her hands to the spindle,…" Proverbs 31:19

God has blessed you with creative ability. This ability enables you to take on various tasks as they arise. In this section you will learn how to thread a needle and sew on a button. The instructions are below. However, it is important that you first ask for permission before beginning any sewing project; sewing projects use many sharp items like needles, pins and scissors so supervision is required.

How to Thread a Needle

Select the thread color needed to match the fabric you are working with

Unwind the thread to match the length of your arm and cut close to the spool

Use this edge since it is a fresh cut to push through the eye of the needle (be patient with yourself especially if you have never done this before; threading a needle does take practice, but you can do it)

Pull the thread through the eye of the needle until the ends of the thread are even and make a knot; the knot will keep the thread from coming out of the needle and help you in your sewing project

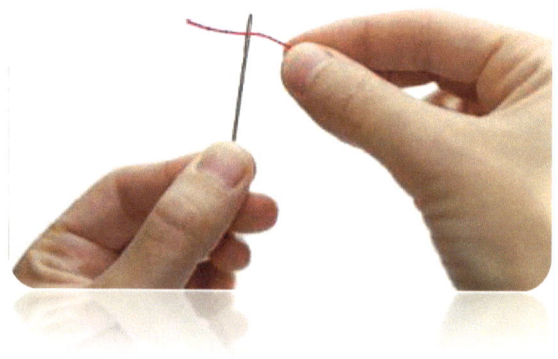

How to Sew on a Button

When a button falls off, be sure to place it somewhere safe so you can sew it back onto your clothing. Many times you will notice when a button is loose before it comes off. If you reinforce the button at this time, it will save you time later and also prevent the button from falling off and getting lost.

> Place the button on the area where you want to attach it. Holding the button in place, push the needle through the wrong side of the fabric and the buttonhole, pulling through until the knot prevents any more pulling (this will put the needle on the right side of the fabric).
>
> Next, push the needle through another hole across from the buttonhole the thread is coming from (this will put the needle on the wrong side of the fabric where you started from).
>
> Repeat the above instructions alternating the buttonholes until the button is firmly attached to the fabric.
>
> Once firmly attached, bring the needle through a button hole.
>
> Using the thread, push the needle underneath the alternating thread and make a knot.
>
> Using scissors, cut off the excess thread and place the used needle and thread on the spool or in a pin cushion (do not leave it out since needles easily fall to the floor and someone could get hurt).
>
> Put sewing materials away (keep all of your sewing items in the same place so you will always know where they are; you can use a shoe box and decorate it if you like).

Chapter 8
Preparation, Never Lost Time

The QNT and Good Stewardship

Through skillful and godly wisdom is a house (a life, a home, a family) built, and by understanding it is established [on a sound and good foundation], and by knowledge shall its chambers [of every area] be filled with all precious and pleasant riches. Proverbs 24:3-4 (AMP)

As a QNT, you must know that preparation is never lost time. It's been said that success happens when opportunity meets a prepared person. I want you to be prepared for every opportunity imaginable. Here are some areas we will discuss in this chapter:

- Reading, Reading, Reading…
- Always being a Student
- Money, Money, Money…
- How to Prepare for an Interview
- Dressing for Success
- Time Management

Always a Student

Take hold of my instructions; don't let them go. Guard them, for they are the key to life.
Proverbs 4:13 NLT

Ladies, you have the opportunity to live life without regret so read, read, read.

As a QNT, speaking and communicating effectively is vitally important to your success. People will judge you privately based on the scope of your vocabulary and your ability to use words skillfully. Yes, I know the scripture says judge not and you will not be judged. But the reality is, people will judge you even though they may never say a word to you directly.

I want you to be well prepared for life, and all that it has to offer, therefore, I suggest that you spend 30 minutes a day reading. Read books and articles that stimulate you intellectually. This will force you to read with a dictionary nearby and which in turn will help you to build your vocabulary.

You are well prepared for life when you have a strong foundation of reading and you have a wide array of words in you to use at will. QNT read daily!

Your days of traditional learning will eventually come to an end, whether after college or graduate school. But never stop learning and understanding new disciplines in life. Please know that all QNTs must be educated. Being illiterate is not an option. Why, because in this day and age life and the opportunities it affords are more limited for the person who has minimal education. Remember, you are here to glorify God and fulfill His purpose for your life. So God wants you to be a well-rounded, well-spoken, educated QNT who can take advantage of the opportunities He has for you. Continue to learn even after completing your traditional education. Many times, you will come across people who are in the field of work that you are in or that you desire to be in and learning for you can take place. You can become their mentee and allow them to be your mentor and they will help you move from where you are to where you would desire to be. It is during these times that you want to take in their words of wisdom and be receptive to their teaching because after all, they are where you desire to be.

Money, Money, Money

As a QNT it is important that you understand money and how it works. In this particular section, I've added on further information from my previous book to help you to be a good steward over the resources God blesses you with.

The scripture says to tell those who are rich in this world not to trust in their riches but in the living God. Always remember that God is your SOURCE.

You can learn very important principles about money. First, your self-worth is not measured by the amount of money you possess. Material items are nice, but they are not character building items. You must understand that money is one tool that God uses to allow His children to enjoy life.

Good stewards are people who realize that it is their duty to be responsible and not wasteful with the finances God supplies in their life. You might think; how do I do that?

Here are a few things to remember when you are handling large or small amounts of money:

- ❖ God gave you the money you have therefore He is your boss; impress Him.

- ❖ It is a privilege to work for God and manage money in a way that pleases Him.
- ❖ Before you spend money or give it away, think about what God wants.
- ❖ God brings you happiness, not the money He gave you to manage.
- ❖ It is your responsibility to make a profit with God's money so invest wisely.
- ❖ Before you can see your money grow, you have to sow (tithes and offerings)
- ❖ To tithe is to give back to God 10% off the top of what He gave to you. Tithe means tenth (Malachi 3:9-10)
- ❖ To give offerings is to give anything above your regular tithes (2 Corinthians 9:6-8)
- ❖ A good steward always saves money for future needs and desires
- ❖ Pay bills on time and review each invoice before you submit it to creditors
- ❖ Put money away for emergencies (this is not your savings)

How to Balance a Check Book

As a QNT, one day you will have a checking account and be responsible for keeping that account balanced. To do so, there are a couple of things you must know.

The bank gives you an organizer with your checks; this is called a check register.

This organizer gives you a place to keep track of the activity in your account.

What are activities? Activities are your deposits, withdrawals, fees and any other charges to your account.

Write down in your register whenever:

You deposit money in your checking account

You write a check

You use your debit card

You deduct a fee that the bank charges

You withdraw money from your account

The key is to write down your transactions at the moment they happen and not try to remember to fill it in later. It is very easy to forget to write in the times you use your debit card. It may seem like a lot of work but you need the information to balance your account. You can check your account balance on-line and think you have more money than you really have by forgetting transactions that have not been processed.

Codes used to balance your check register:

Number- refers to the check number

DC for Debit Card

ATM for a cash withdrawal

D for Deposit

T - Transfer to your savings account, etc.

Date - Always record the date of anything you do

Description of transaction - Nails done etc.

Payment/Debit - Here you record the amounts of money going out of your account

Deposit/Credit - Here you record the amounts of money coming into your account

As you enter each item, date it. Then in the far right column, either add or subtract to reach a new total. Make yourself record information at the time you write the check, use the ATM, or make the deposit. Two days later, you won't remember what you did.

Today, checks and debit card transactions are debited from a checking account very quickly. If you write a check and do not have the money in your account you "bounce" a check.

This is a No-No for "QNT. The bank returns the check to you unpaid, and the bank will charge you a hefty fee. Usually if this happens you will have written several checks and you get a fee for each one. It adds up! If you have a debit card on the account, it will be deactivated.

A Word about Credit

Owe no man anything but love. Romans 13:8

Financial freedom is God's best for the QNT. As you are developing and when you become of age (18) you will be bombarded with all types of credit offers. REFUSE THEM. I REPEAT, REFUSE THEM.

Credit and Debit is a trap to get you entangled in the system. The scripture clearly says that the borrower is servant (slave) to the lender. This means that for every credit card you hold that institution will own you in a financial sense.

Learn to save your money and pay cash for the things you desire. This philosophy of thinking will keep you financially free of the world's system. This will mean that you will need to learn to delay self-gratification. You can start now by only purchasing things you have saved the money to buy. If you don't have it, then don't purchase it. I know this is easier said than done but if you master this discipline and philosophy now; you will in the long run be a very blessed lady.

You say, how will I get a car? You get a car by starting now to save for it and pay cash.

For the sake of instruction we will discuss the credit score.

A credit score is a number representing the credit worthiness of a person; the likelihood the person will pay his or her bills. Lenders, such as banks and credit card companies, use credit scores to evaluate the potential risk posed by lending money to consumers.

Credit scores range from

760-850 **Excellent**

700-759 **Very Good**

660-699 **Good**

620-659 **Not Good**

580-619 **Poor**

500-579 **Very Poor**

The higher your credit score, the more credit worthy lenders feel that you are.

I realize this information may be a little premature for you but remember this is to be a reference tool to guide you through your transitioning years.

(Above information on credit is collected from google.com)

How to Prepare for an Interview

Preparation is truly never lost time. One of the biggest mistakes people make prior to going on an interview is not preparing for it. Remember if you're looking for a job, you must do everything in your power to have a successful interview and to make a good lasting impression so that you maximize your chances of being offered the position. Below are some suggestions on how to land the job you desire.

<u>What are You Going to Wear?</u>

> **1 Timothy 2:9** *New Living Translation (NLT)*
> *And I want women to be modest in their appearance. They should wear decent and appropriate clothing and not draw attention to themselves by the way they fix their hair or by wearing gold or pearls or expensive clothes.*

This is not a question that you want to ignore. You should never underestimate the power of the first impression – it matters! Everything matters…never think that the smallest details will go unnoticed. The interviewer is looking for the best candidate for their organization. So when dressing for an interview, remember, less is best. You never want to be flashy; be modest, keep it simple.

You should always dress for success. Dress for where you are going in life…Dress for Success! Business suits are always the best choice for interviews; either a pant suit or a dress suit. Never assume that not wearing stockings, hosiery or wearing open toe shoes are appropriate if you live in a hot climate; the best choice is

always wearing the appropriate hosiery and closed toed dress shoes for an interview.

- ❖ Remember to polish your shoes.
- ❖ Always have an extra pair of stockings on hand, just in case you run your stockings on your way to the interview.

Modesty vs. the Culture

Modesty would include you covering up tattoos and taking out any body piercings that you will most likely live to regret getting. What most young people fail to realize is that tattoos and body piercings have been the reason behind them not landing a second interview or receiving the job. Tattoos may seem like a way for you to express yourself or your undying loyalty to someone; but it usually becomes a costly mistake that you can't easily erase in adulthood, not to mention the fact that it will cause you to miss a lot of great opportunities in life. So if you don't have any tattoos, keep it that way. You are already different. Remember that you are fearfully and wonderfully made by God, and there will never be another you! You express yourself by being who God created you to be! You are an original - His original.

Hair Styles and Nails

When going on an interview you should always stay on the conservative side. Your hair should be washed and well maintained. Outlandish hair colors and Mo-hawks are by no means what you want to wear for an interview. Remember modesty does matter!

There are only two ways to wear nail polish, and that's on or off. Chipped nail polish is not acceptable for an interview; you are better off removing it. When going on an interview, you should wear one color on your nails. I would suggest sticking with colors that don't draw too much attention. Stay away from colors such as green, blue, purple, hot pink, etc. And make sure you cut your nails down low or to a medium length.

Do a Drive By

You should do a 'drive by' to the location of your interview the day before. If your interview is on a week day, then your 'drive by' should be done on a week day, and it would be good if you could do it around the same time of your interview. Traffic differs from the time and day of the week. For instance, a Saturday interview might have fewer vehicles on the road, as opposed to a weekday. When you arrive at the location, go into the building find out where you have to arrive for the interview. You never know if you might need to catch the elevator to the 13th floor, and wouldn't you like to know before-hand if the building has one slow elevator prior to the day of your interview, rather than the day of?

When Should I Arrive

A good rule of thumb to follow is that on time, is late. You should allow yourself 30 minutes to arrive prior to your interview. That will allow you extra time to use the restroom if you need to, review your notes, or just to calm down. Your being on time lets an employer know that time is important to you, because it is most definitely important to them. So after you get the position, you should continue to practice to arrive at least 15 minutes prior to your start time, until it becomes a habit. This is one of those good habits to have.

Resume'

A resume' is basically a self-assessment of yourself, and your accomplishments. Most employers like for you to get to the point, so be detailed and accurate. A resume' that is longer than one page could hurt you, especially at your age.

For instance, if you have had 8 different jobs in the past, it could tell an employer that you aren't consistent or dedicated to a company; or that you have gotten fired on more than one occasion.

You want to make sure that your resume' is free of grammatical or spelling errors. So take your time and re-read your resume' slowly. It's always good for you to have an extra pair of fresh eyes to review it for you also. So ask one of your parents/mentors or friends to proof read it for you.

What do you know about the Company and the position you are interviewing for?

You should always research the company that you are interviewing for. You can 'google' anything in today's society. Research, read, and write down questions. Do you know why you want to work for that organization? Or do you just want a job? Does that company have a history of illegal actions? What are some questions that you might have for the interviewer? Do they have a high turnover of employees? These are some things that you will find out if you do your research.

Thank You Card/Note

After the interview you want to immediately drop a thank you note in the mail to the person(s) who conducted the interview. Some interviews are conducted by more than one person; and a thank you card should be mailed to everyone individually. So make sure you get a business card from the person(s) at the end of the interview. The note is basically sent to thank them for taking the time to interview you. Sending a thank you card or note is a good way to give your potential employers a great lasting impression of you.

Religion/Politics

When interviewing, you will want to stay away from any religious or political views that you may have. Remember you are there to provide that company a service, by which you will be compensated for. If there is something in your job description that requires you to perform a function that is against God's way of you conducting yourself, then you should be prepared to walk away knowing that job is not the position for you and vice versa. With this said, the attitude of a QNT regarding potential positions is that you are to pray to God about future jobs or positions. God knows what's best for you and He will grant you the desires of your heart if you bring them to Him. But what's also great, is that He will protect you from things that will harm you once you are in relationship with Him. Remember at the beginning of this book I mentioned that your relationship with the Father is the most important relationship to cultivate. And all other relationships will grow from your relationship with the Father.

This also includes bosses and people put in authority over you. Pray that the position will still allow you to attend services when the house of God is open for Worship.

Time Management

Ephesians 5:15-17 Message
So watch your step. Use your head. Make the most of every chance you get. These are desperate times!
Don't live carelessly, unthinkingly. Make sure you understand what the Master wants.

Time = life; therefore, waste your time and waste your life, or master your time and master your life.
~Alan Lakein

As a QNT, time management is not just important, it is imperative to be able to navigate through life successfully. Without the proper use of time, life can be chaotic and even stressful. However, if you master the skill of time management at this stage in your life, you will develop into a very productive member of society.

Time Management is simply the ability to control your time.

Everyone is given 24 hours in a day. The proper use of time is what helps a person to accomplish many tasks and be the most productive. Here is a breakdown of a typical day for most QNT's. It can vary based on individual situations.

<u>24 Hour Break Down of Time</u>

8 hours – Sleep

8 hours – School

1 hour – Commute Time to school (round trip)

30 minutes Personal Hygiene Time (Bath, Shower etc)

30 minutes – Eating (between breakfast and dinner)

2 hours - Extra Curricular Activities etc.

1 hour – Homework (varies)

2-3 hours – Other. With foundational things in place like the above list, most QNT's have 3 to 4 hours every school day to manage. The weekends would vary greatly with much more time on your hands. To manage your time well, you will need a calendar or a planner and later maybe even a PDA also known as a Professional Digital Assistant. Creating a daily checklist of things to do is also very beneficial in being productive and managing your time.

On or in a calendar, write out scheduled activities, events, homework, chores, test and projects. Doing this and keeping it current will eliminate stress. Stress is the feeling of being overwhelmed with the responsibility of handling many things at one time. As a QNT, properly managing your time can be greatly beneficial. The most important factor is getting all of those responsibilities out of your head and onto paper. The persons who do this as a way of life are highly developed in time management.

Make time your friend

Time can be your best friend or your worst enemy. Make time your friend by being proactive. To be proactive means to prepare in advance for all of your responsibilities and activities. Time becomes your enemy if you are a procrastinator. A procrastinator is someone who waits until the last minute to get things done. The procrastinator will always find that there is never enough time. Why, because they habitually wait until the last minute and things ALWAYS take longer to complete. When this happens, time becomes your enemy and it becomes a race against the clock.

Time Management Tips

- Use a Planner Daily
- Keep your planner current
- Write activities, homework, test dates, chores, events etc. in your planner.
- Review daily activities
- Use a to do task list
- Plan ahead using your planner
- Prioritize to complete the most important projects

Planning ahead using your calendar will help you to be a better student and can prevent cramming. For example, if you wrote in your planner, "Test Friday" and you study a little everyday in preparation for the test, you will be well prepared for that test compared to not writing it down and studying only the night before the test. QNT's are well prepared and manage time well.

Chapter 9

Dare to Dream

Dreaming big requires imagination. It's funny how God used dreams to show people His plans for their future. Limited thinking hinders and restricts us from accomplishing great things in life. In Mark *9:23 Amp Jesus said…all things can be (are possible) to him who believes!* Dreams are possible. Don't limit your life by failing to dream, and believing that dreams don't come true. Your dreams are linked to your destiny. God gave Joseph a dream, and his dreams eventually all came to pass.

God is limitless; and his Word is powerful. The bible says in Isaiah 55:11 (AMP) *So shall My word be that goes forth out of My mouth: it shall not return to Me void [without producing any effect, useless], but it shall accomplish that which I please and purpose, and it shall prosper in the thing for which I sent it.*

Throughout the Bible and throughout the ages God has been restricted from moving in our lives because we didn't have faith to take Him at his Word. God can't lie. The scripture says in Numbers 23:19 (NLT) *God is not a man, so he does not lie. He is not human, so he does not change his mind. Has he ever spoken and failed to act? Has he ever promised and not carried it through?*

As a QNT, you need to dare to dream and allow the Holy Spirit to lead and to guide you. God has a purpose for you individually, that is why you can't be consumed by watching others. Yes cheer them on in their success, while at the same time understanding that God has something great for you to do. God wants you successful so you can advance His Kingdom, and positively touch and change lives by His power and guidance.

My heart is for you to fully know God's will for your life and to complete your God given assignment. So dream QNT, and DREAM BIG!

Know that God loves you, and I love you too –

Stephanie Denise Garrett

Sample Vision Board

Dream House

Dream Car

Vision

Fashion

Kingdom Building

Career

(Picture of you and your dream family)

Friends   Dream

www.ingramcontent.com/pod-product-compliance
Lightning Source LLC
Chambersburg PA
CBHW042330150426
43194CB00001B/7